8/14

D1499359

Machines at Work

Trucks

by Cari Meister

Bullfrog Books

Ideas for Parents and Teachers

Bullfrog Books let children practice nonfiction reading at the earliest reading levels. Repetition, familiar words, and photo labels support early readers.

Before Reading

- Discuss the cover photo. What does it tell them?
- Look at the picture glossary together. Read and discuss the words.

Read the Book

- "Walk" through the book and look at the photos. Let the child ask questions. Point out the photo labels.
- Read the book to the child, or have him or her read independently.

After Reading

- Prompt the child to think more. Ask: What kind of trucks do you see where you live? What kind of jobs do they do?

Bullfrog Books are published by Jump!
5357 Penn Avenue South
Minneapolis, MN 55419
www.jumplibrary.com

Library of Congress Cataloging-in-Publication Data
Meister, Cari.
  Trucks / by Cari Meister.
    pages cm. -- (Bullfrog books. Machines at work)
  Includes bibliographical references and index.
  Summary: "This photo-illustrated book for early readers tells about many different trucks and how they are used"-- Provided by publisher.
  Audience: Age 5.
  Audience: Grades K to grade 3.
  ISBN 978-1-62031-049-6 (hardcover : alk. paper) --
ISBN 978-1-62496-061-1 (ebook)
  1. Trucks--Juvenile literature. I. Title.
  TL230.15.M453 2014
  629.224--dc23
                                        2012042022

Photo credits:
Alamy, 1, 6–7, 10–11, 18–19, 23tl; Dreamstime, 5, 12, 20, 23tr; Shutterstock, cover, 3, 4, 6, 9, 11, 14, 15t, 15b, 21, 22, 23tr, 23br, 24; Superstock, 8, 17

Series Editor: Rebecca Glaser
Book Editor: Patrick Perish
Series Designer: Ellen Huber

Printed in the United States of America at Corporate Graphics in North Mankato, Minnesota.
4-2013 / PO 1003
10 9 8 7 6 5 4 3 2 1

Table of Contents

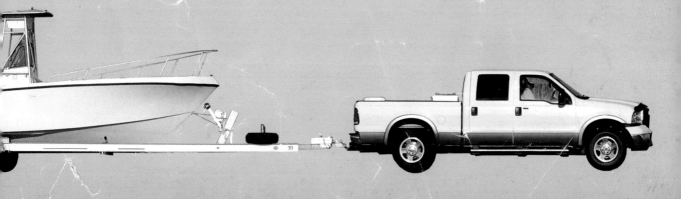

Trucks at Work

Here comes
a truck!

Trucks are powerful.

Their big engines help them go.

A pick-up truck carries cargo in its bed.

The driver sits in the cab.

bed

cab

A big rig carries food in its trailer.
It brings food to stores.

trailer

69 70 71 72 73 74 75 76 77 78 79

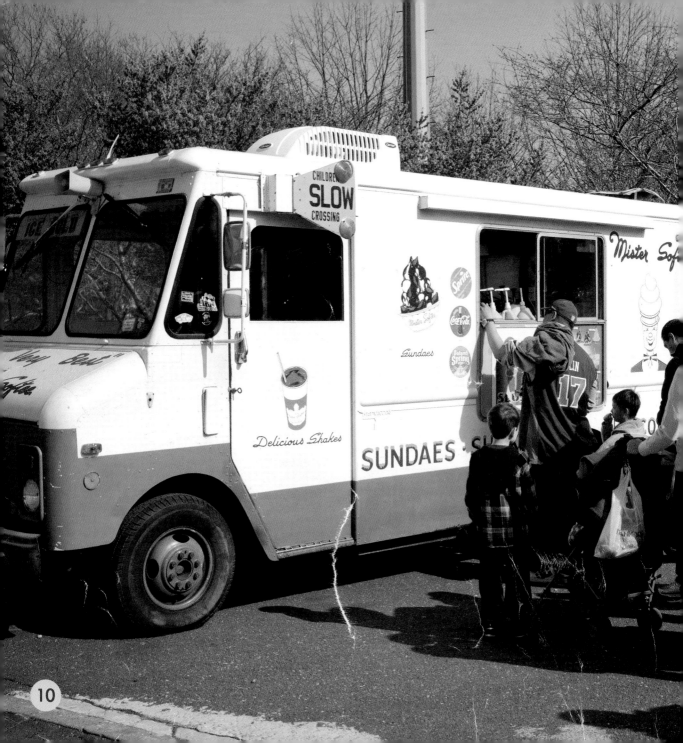

Ding! Ding!
An ice cream truck
brings treats.

It has a freezer inside.

A garbage truck collects trash.

hopper

It is crushed in the hopper.

A house is on fire.

A fire truck comes.

hydrant

14

The hose hooks
to the hydrant.

Now it can spray water.

A car crashed.

A tow truck
pulls it away.

An armored truck
carries money.

It is bulletproof.

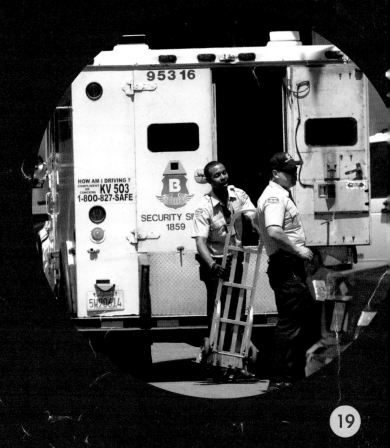

A monster truck has big tires.
People come to watch.

What a great show!

Parts of a Truck

engine
A motor that powers the truck.

cab
The place where the driver sits.

bed
The flat area on which goods can be carried.

Picture Glossary

armor
A metal covering that protects something.

hopper
The part of a garbage truck where trash is stored.

cargo
Any sort of goods being hauled.

trailer
The back part of a truck that carries cargo.

Index

To Learn More

Learning more is as easy as 1, 2, 3.

1) Go to www.factsurfer.com

2) Enter "truck" into the search box.

3) Click the "Surf" button to see a list of websites.

) With factsurfer.com, finding more information is just a click away.